Original title:
Coconut Beach Tales

Copyright © 2025 Creative Arts Management OÜ
All rights reserved.

Author: Vivian Laurent
ISBN HARDBACK: 978-1-80581-502-0
ISBN PAPERBACK: 978-1-80581-029-2
ISBN EBOOK: 978-1-80581-502-0

Breezes and Island Epiphanies

A crab in a hat wears shades of bright,
He dances on sand, what a curious sight.
The seagulls all laugh, they squawk and they tease,
While the sun pours down, just as sweet as a breeze.

A tourist with snacks, quite clumsy and loud,
Trips over a dolphin, attracts quite a crowd.
He shouts, "No, it's fine! I'm a fish out of sea!"
But the dolphin just splashes, in fits of pure glee.

The turtles all gossip, on logs by the shore,
"Did you hear about Larry? He swam to the floor!"
They chuckle and snicker at Larry's great flub,
He thought he was swimming, but landed in a tub.

Two parrots engage in a squawking debate,
On whether the snacks should be salty or straight.
One says, "More pineapple, it's tasty and sweet!"
The other just squawks, "No, give me a treat!"

Life in Sun-kissed Shores

Seagulls sing a silly song,
While crabs dance along the throng.
Sunbathers nap with funny hats,
Turtles chuckle, 'Ain't this spats?'

Ice cream cones melt in the heat,
A squirrel thinks it's a treat.
Kids chase waves, splash and scream,
While dolphins jump and steal the dream.

The Eco of Ocean Whispers

Shells tell tales of days gone by,
In the sea, the fish just sigh.
Starfish play peek-a-boo with sand,
While seaweed jigs, it's quite unplanned.

Whales hum tunes in ocean's choir,
Mermaids giggle, never tired.
Crabs hold parties beneath the tide,
With sea cucumbers as their guide.

Chasing Shadows on the Sand

Footprints lead to nowhere fast,
As kites fly judging from the past.
Flip-flops flip; a toddler falls,
Laughter echoes through the calls.

Sandcastles leaning, kings of hopes,
While ice cream's gone, we draw the slopes.
Chasing shadows, fun-filled race,
A seagull steals your lunch—what grace!

Coral Secrets and Hidden Dreams

Fish wear ties, oh what a sight,
Coral dances in the light.
Octopuses dress up for show,
As sea turtles say, 'Let's go slow!'

Bubbles popping, voices cheer,
Underwater tickles, never fear.
Day ends with a sunset spree,
All is goofy, wild, and free.

The Rhythm of the Waves

The waves are in a race, oh dear,
They splash on my toes, bring hearty cheer.
A seagull swoops, steals my snack,
I chase it down, but it won't look back.

The tide rolls in, I grab my float,
A crab scuttles past, it's quite the goat.
I jump and giggle, he poses bold,
While the sun paints the sky with tones of gold.

Laughter Under the Canopy

Under leafy green, the shade feels nice,
But watch out, there's a ant-sized heist!
A picnic spread, pure bliss and delight,
Till ants form a line; it's a funny sight!

With sticky fingers, we munch away,
The mango juice makes us sway and play.
A monkey swings down; he joins the spree,
Swiping a sandwich—oh, it's up a tree!

Dreams on Salty Breezes

The salty breeze tickles our nose,
It sways our dreams like a flower grows.
But wait, oh look! A hat takes flight,
Chasing it down is such a sight!

Flip-flops flying, laughter cries out,
The running is funny; there's no doubt.
We dive for the hat, stumble and fall,
And end up in sand—oh, who saw that call?

The Dance of the Drifting Clouds

Clouds puff and dance like silly puffs,
They play peek-a-boo, and that's just tough!
A rain drop teases, then joins the play,
Splashing around, it's a wild ballet!

With giggles galore in a sunbeam's glow,
We twirl and leap, the world moves slow.
Grab your friend, let's spin around,
Under fluffy clouds, our joy is found!

Sunset Serenade in Paradise

The sun dips low, wearing its gold,
A crab on a mission, oh behold!
A flip-flop flies, a chase begins,
Fish laugh hard, let the games spin.

Seagulls squawk with a cheeky grin,
As a turtle dances, let's join in!
Cocktail spills, what a wild brew,
And all the fish are giggling too.

Island Echoes and Sandy Stories

A parrot jokes in vibrant tones,
While kids build castles, using phones.
A beach ball bounces, sails a kite,
The laughter echoes into the night.

Shells wear sunglasses, oh so bright,
While sand ninjas spar, what a sight!
Tides tell tales with bubbly glee,
As doggy paddles, splashing free.

Songs from the Surf

Waves crash in, a splashy tune,
Dolphins flip beneath the moon.
A ukulele joins the fun,
As starfish tap to beats on run.

Jellyfish jive, with a twisty flair,
While seaweed boogies, without a care.
The surfboard's riddled with sticky sand,
As everyone dances, hand in hand.

Mangoes and Melodies

Mangoes drop with a juicy thud,
As roosters crow, proud in the mud.
A smoothie spills, laughter roars,
While ants march in for fruity scores.

Banana peels invite a slide,
As tourists tumble, oh what pride!
The blender hums a merry song,
And we all sing along, all day long.

Whispers of the Tide

Upon the shore, the waves do prance,
Crabs in tiny pants join the dance.
Seagulls squawk a merry tune,
While beach balls bounce under the moon.

A sun hat flies, what a sight!
It lands on a dog, causing a fright.
Sandy toes wiggle with glee,
As sunscreen battles with a bee.

Secrets Beneath the Palms

Beneath the palms, a secret lies,
A jellyfish with googly eyes.
It tells the tale of a sailor's hat,
And how he trained a lazy cat.

Two starfish argue who's more bright,
One claims it kissed a dolphin's light.
The other boasts of tales of woe,
When waves swept in, and it lost its glow.

Sandcastles and Moonbeams

In the twilight, dreams arise,
Sandcastles spark like childhood lies.
With buckets high, the laughter spills,
As seaweed dons a crown, it thrills.

A crab conducts a zany band,
While kids rejoice, it's truly grand.
Moonbeams twinkle in delight,
As treasures found glow in the night.

Shadows of the Shoreline

Shadows play beneath the sun,
A clam decides it's time for fun.
It wears a shell, all decked in flair,
And dances like it just don't care.

A tour guide parrot shouts, "Not so fast!"
"Don't eat that sand, it's not a feast!"
With laughter echoing all around,
The best of times in joy is found.

Enchanted Shores

On sandy banks, a crab did dance,
He clutched a hat, looking for chance.
A seagull swooped, what a sight!
The crab yelled, 'That's my hat, take flight!'

With waves that rolled, so loud and free,
A fish slipped by, as sleek as a bee.
It winked at kids with ice cream treats,
'Who needs your cones? I've got my beats!'

The Call of the Dunes

A hermit crab with a shell of flair,
Mimicked a dog, it licked the air.
Tourists giggled, what a show!
'Hey, that's my beach ball, don't you know?'

An old man tan, with a parrot wise,
Taught the bird to mimic his cries.
'Polly want a drink?' the bird would squawk,
While everyone lined up for sun and talk.

Spirits of the Island

Beneath a tree, a monkey played,
With sunglasses on, it mislaid.
It tossed a coconut up with glee,
'Watch out below, it's raining free!'

A lizard laughed, as quick as light,
Chasing the monkey, a silly sight.
Together they spun, in merry chase,
These island spirits showed such grace.

Sunset Serenades

At dusk, the sky wore shades of pink,
A group of frogs began to blink.
They croaked a tune, oh what a sound,
As dancing fish jumped all around!

A night parade led by a crab,
With other sea folks, ready to blab.
'Join us now, it's nothing but fun!
The moon's our disco, let's run, run, run!'

The Journey of Forgotten Shells

On sandy shores, the shells do sigh,
Each one a story, under the sky.
Tossed by waves, they sometimes roll,
Lost to the fun of a beachy stroll.

A crab in a shell, thinks he's so grand,
Pretending to rule the whole sea strand.
But once a wave gives him a shove,
He scurries away, empty of love.

Seagulls cackle, stealing my fries,
While a clam simply glares with surprise.
The sun's blazing bright, so I take a dip,
My snorkel and fins, it's time for a trip.

I find a lost flip-flop, what a great catch!
It's giant and yellow, quite the mismatch.
Yet here on the shore, with laughter and glee,
The weirdest of treasures belong solely to me.

Embrace of the Horizon

The sun dips low, a laugh in the sky,
A seagull flaps by, in sweet good-bye.
I wave to a dolphin; he winks with a flip,
As I'm jumping the waves in a bright yellow strip.

Tangled in seaweed, my friend takes a dive,
Claiming the ocean makes him feel alive.
But with every splash comes a squeaky surprise,
He surfaces all green, oh, what a guise!

Shells whisper secrets with each passing tide,
As if they're in on the fun with my ride.
The horizon beckons with tales so absurd,
Of mermaids who giggle, oh haven't you heard?

A sandcastle stands, topped with a spray,
While kids build their kingdoms and call it their day.
With every new wave, laughter ignites,
As we embrace together these silly delights.

Coastal Chronicles

In the morning glow, with coffee in hand,
A pelican lands, ever so grand.
He snags my bagel, what a cheeky feat,
I laugh as he waddles, thinking he's neat.

A beach ball bounces, it flies past my face,
Caught in a tussle, we're in quite a race.
With sand stuck to sunscreen, I tumble and roll,
The giggles erupt, taking back control.

The tide steals my towel as I chase it away,
Yet in this wild chaos, I choose to stay.
As laughter erupts from the kids on the shore,
The memories weave tales I'll always adore.

With each tide that turns, the stories unfold,
Of treasures and laughter more precious than gold.
So here's to the antics, the joy that will last,
In this dance of the waves, our worries are cast.

Tides of Time

As the moon rises high, a wise old crab grins,
He tells of the tides and where laughter begins.
Each splash tells a joke, a riddle so bright,
When sea foam tickles, it feels just right.

Old fishing boats bob, like ducks on a line,
While a dog makes a splash, thinking he's fine.
The catch of the day? A sandpiper's snack,
Half stolen, half shared, as they dance in a pack.

Beach umbrellas spin in a chaotic ballet,
With wind-tossed towels shouting, "Come out to play!"
The sun takes a bow, it's the end of the show,
But the stories we harvested will surely still glow.

So let's spin our tales, as the tides ebb and flow,
With laughter and fun as our day starts to slow.
In this merry dance where time seems absurd,
Every splash a memory, each giggle conferred.

The Heartbeat of the Harbor

The pelicans dive with a plop,
While the seagulls squawk and hop.
A crab nods, with one big claw,
As tourists giggle at the bizarre law.

Children chase the waves with glee,
While beach balls roll from tree to sea.
A dog with shades and coconut in tow,
Thinks he's the captain of the show.

A fisherman tossed his bait with flair,
But it landed right on someone's hair!
Laughter erupts from every side,
As the tide comes in, oh, what a ride!

And when the sun begins to set,
The harbor hums with no regret.
Stories shared, and jokes anew,
As laughter lingers like the view.

Treasures of a Thousand Tides

The treasure chest is full of shells,
And jellyfish jiggle, the harbor yells!
A starfish sits, quite nonchalant,
As beachcombers search for a shiny font.

Sandcastles rise, facing the breeze,
Each bucket full creates a tease.
But a rogue wave comes, with a silly splash,
Toppling towers in a mighty crash!

A crab scuttles past, in a race with a kite,
The owners of both, sprawled out in delight.
"Who's the faster?" they shout with cheer,
As laughter rings, louder than any beer.

Mysterious rocks hold secrets untold,
As mermaids giggle, or so I'm told.
With treasures found, all smile wide,
As the sun waves goodbye on its glide.

The Whisper of Warm Winds

The winds swipe playfully at hats,
As laughter dances with snaky chats.
A lobster sings, though it's quite absurd,
While a beachgoer happily strums a chord.

Warm winds tickle those on the sand,
As sunscreen flies from a clumsy hand.
A frisbee sails and plops in a drink,
Making everyone pause, and think.

Flip-flops squeak like a marching band,
A sunburned nose leads the sandy strand.
While the smell of barbecue fills the air,
Someone's hair catches fire from a flare!

The warm winds whisper tales of fun,
With sandy kisses from the rolling run.
As night falls down, and stories are spun,
It's laughter that dances, and never is done.

A Canvas of Sea and Sky

On the horizon, colors clash and play,
Like artists gone wild in broad daylight.
The sea laughs back with foamy fray,
Dancing to the rhythm of pure delight.

Umbrellas flutter like big blooms bright,
As sunbathers expand their limbs like birds.
A perfect canvas, but oh, what a sight,
As sunscreen gets splattered, stirring words!

A couple tries yoga, but here comes a wave,
Sending them tumbling, oh what a rave!
With giggles erupting like popcorn in air,
Curtains of laughter billow everywhere.

As the sun drips low, and colors gleam,
The sea whispers secrets in a dreamy beam.
With a wink from the sky, and a chuckle or two,
Here's a masterpiece, created anew!

Stories in the Surf

The waves crash with giggles, oh what a sight,
A crab in a tuxedo, in morning's light.
Seagulls squawk jokes, they're punny and loud,
As fish then take bets, under seaweed shroud.

A kid with a bucket, his treasure's a shoe,
He claims it's a pirate's, oh what a view!
Turtles in shades, lounging with flair,
Sandcastles that wobble, but nobody cares.

The sun starts to set, with a wink and a grin,
A dolphin does flips, just to fit in.
Folks gather round, for a tale of the tides,
With laughter and cheer, as the fun collides.

The day wraps in splendor, a bright orange hue,
As night falls, we share stories with the crew.
The ocean's our stage, full of whimsy and glee,
In the surf, all our laughter, forever will be.

Serenade of the Seafoam

A starfish with dreams of becoming a star,
Plays ukulele, strumming near and far.
Jellyfish twirl in elegant grace,
While clownfish swim by, a painted-up face.

The seafoam dances, a light-hearted jig,
As octopuses juggle, it's quite the big gig.
A blowfish inflates, declares he's the best,
In this underwater ball, who needs all the rest?

A pelican with swagger lands on the dock,
Wears shades and a hat, oh, what a talk!
Tales of the waves drench the night's sweet air,
With laughter and music, we banish despair.

We're serenading seashells, under the moon,
The night sings a tune, oh, not too soon.
With joy in the foam, and stars high above,
This ocean of laughter, pure friendship and love.

Footprints in Golden Sand

Footprints line up like a wobbly train,
A dog with a stick thinks they're all in vain.
The tide comes to laugh, washes traces away,
While the sun chases clouds, in its playful display.

A crab races off, it's a high-speed chase,
With runners behind, it's a comical race.
Flip-flops go flying as people all trip,
Chasing sandcastles, oh, let's not skip!

Children are giggling, squeals fill the air,
As they splash in the shallows without a care.
Moms build a fortress, while daddies conspire,
With water balloons, it's their ultimate fire!

The golden sands sparkle, as laughter abounds,
Each footstep a story, in whimsical sounds.
With friends all around, in this sun-soaked land,
Each moment's a treasure, where memories stand.

Emerald Waters and Night Skies

Emerald waters are sparkling bright,
While mermaids sing tales to the stars tonight.
A boat full of friends drifts along for the ride,
With ice cream in hand, and the moon as our guide.

The seagulls swoosh down, performing their act,
One steals a sandwich, a bold little fact.
The sky begins twinkling, all dreamy and fine,
As we share silly stories, with laughter entwined.

A fish with a top hat and monocle too,
Tells jokes about clams; oh, what a view!
The dolphins are dancing, splashing delight,
In our ocean of fun, every moment's just right.

As stars twinkle playfully, splashes abound,
The echo of laughter is the sweet, soothing sound.
In emerald waters, and under night's gleam,
We weave all our tales into one dreamy theme.

Lolling at the Lagoon's Edge

On a rock, I sat with cheer,
A crab dashed by, I lost my beer.
It waved its claws, gave me a wink,
I watched it dance, forgot to think.

The sun above began to fry,
I swatted flies with a mad hi-fi.
A parrot squawked, 'Let's have some fun!'
The beach ball bounced, the day's begun!

My flip-flops flung, oh what a sight,
The tide rolled in, took them outright.
I chased my shoes, what a fine race,
A fish blew bubbles, joined the chase!

So here I laze, with laughter loud,
A sandy friend, an oddball crowd.
Together we bask in sun's soft glow,
The lagoon's edge, what a funny show!

Fables from the Foam

With a splash, the stories rise,
A seagull's tale of sweet surprise.
'Two fish were swimming, side by side,
One saw a net, it tried to hide!'

In salty waves, the tales are spun,
A starfish claimed it's number one.
The seaweed chuckled, 'What do you know?
I'm here to stay, you're just below!'

A hermit crab, in borrowed shells,
Told of his dreams and ocean smells.
He said, 'I'd trade for legs like yours,
But alas, I'm destined for sea floors!'

From foam to foam, each tale does flow,
A chorus of laughter, a mystery show.
So raise your shells, and let's all cheer,
For fables spun, our hearts will steer!

Vintage Views of the Voyage

On a boat, we set our sail,
With a wink and laugh, we'd never fail.
The captain slipped, fell on his hat,
The crew erupted—imagine that!

Old maps all crinkled, stories untold,
A parrot squawked, 'This ship is gold!'
With each big wave, and each small jibe,
We danced with sharks, oh what a vibe!

The treasure hunt was quite a bust,
Just a chest of seashells, crust and rust.
We toasted to riches found in fun,
And tossed a coin to the setting sun.

So here we roam, on ocean wide,
With vintage tales to be our guide.
For in this trip, we've struck it rich,
With laughter loud, and an ocean itch!

Serene Shores and Sunsets

The sun dipped low, a peachy glow,
With sandy toes, we stole the show.
A dog named Bob, he ran in glee,
Chasing his tail—oh, what a spree!

A sunset painted, skies aflame,
While seagulls squawked our names like fame.
We shared our snacks, a feast divine,
With giggles echoing, hearts align.

Tom tried to juggle, three coconuts,
But one went flying, oh what a cut!
The laughter roared, it's hard to rest,
When evening falls, we're truly blessed.

So here we gather, stories unfold,
Under the stars, our hearts are bold.
With serene shores, this night we'll keep,
For fun and joy, in memories deep.

Dance of the Seagulls

On sandy shores they strut around,
With silly squawks, they make no sound.
They flap and hop in wild delight,
As tourists laugh, what a silly sight!

A crab scuttles by, they chase in glee,
Thinking it's a game, oh what a spree!
But crabs just giggle and pinch with flair,
These feathered friends haven't a care!

A daring dive from high above,
A splash, a flail, the crowd in love.
With beach balls flying, they take a swing,
Who knew seagulls could dance and sing!

When the sun sets, they take a bow,
Outrageous moves, we're all saying "Wow!"
With one last flap, they soar away,
Leaving us chuckling at their display.

The Color of Dusk

As daylight fades, the sky turns pink,
The laughter fades, but oh, we think:
What mischief lurks in the twilight glow,
With shadows dancing, stealing the show!

Sandy toes and tangled hair,
All our worries soar in the air.
With every hue, a new prank waits,
Under the canvas, where fun elates!

Seashells whisper secrets, quite the tease,
Telling stories carried by the breeze.
The starfish giggle, the waves just hum,
As twilight tumbles, we await the fun!

So gather 'round as the colors blend,
With silly tales that never end.
In this dusky hue, joy sings aloud,
We'll laugh together, a happy crowd.

Remnants of Forgotten Boats

Old boats lie anchored, silent and still,
With stories tangled in every frill.
They used to sail with laughter and cheer,
Now they rest, hoping someone will steer.

Each barnacle tells of playful tides,
Fish dancing nearby, nowhere to hide.
Once mighty vessels, full of zest,
Now just driftwood, taking a rest.

Waves tickle them, make them sway,
Seaweed drapes in a funny way.
The gulls sit perched, plotting new schemes,
While fishermen snicker, lost in their dreams.

Yet every sunset, they glow with pride,
Remnants of laughter forever tied.
With salty air, they catch a whiff,
Of joyful stories, and the odd mischief.

Memories in the Mist

In morning's mist, the world feels new,
With giggles floating, a playful crew.
The sandcastle towers now sunken low,
Yet laughter whispers, 'We'll still glow!'

A game of tag between the waves,
Secrets hidden in watery caves.
With every splash, a memory's made,
Woven in sunlight, never to fade.

The crickets chirp, the seashells sigh,
Reminding us of days gone by.
With toes in the surf, we'll shout and play,
In the misty morning, joy leads the way!

So raise your cup to the funny times,
To breezy laughs and silly rhymes.
For every giggle, every twist,
Are memories cherished, not to be missed!

The Aroma of Ocean Air

Salty breezes dance around,
With flip-flops lost, they twirl and bound.
Seagulls squawk, they're quite the jest,
As beach snacks vanish, it's a quest.

A crab in shades, with sunblock too,
Dances sideways, what a view!
Laughter lingers in the sun,
While chasing waves, we all just run.

Tanned toes dip in foamy tides,
As jellyfish go on wild rides.
Mango smoothies spill and splash,
We giggle so hard, it's a bash.

Sunset brings the evening's cheer,
With tales of antics, loud and clear.
Under stars, our laughter reigns,
In ocean air, no room for pains.

Calypso Rhythms and Ocean Blues

A twangy tune floats on by,
As people dance, we laugh and sigh.
Bamboo sticks like drums do thump,
While clumsy feet create a clump.

A parrot's squawk steals the show,
With salsa moves that steal the glow.
Fish swim by with silly grins,
As we attempt their twisting spins.

Beach balls bouncing in a race,
Someone yells, "It's all your face!"
With laughter echoing on the shore,
We dance until we can't no more.

Calypso vibes that hit the spot,
As waves keep crashing, never caught.
With ocean blues and silly tunes,
Our hearts sing loud, like summer moons.

Echoes of Abandoned Coves

In sandy nooks where laughter hides,
We stumble upon crabby rides.
An 'abandoned' chair, a treasure found,
Where giggles echo all around.

We play at ghosts of sailors past,
With bucket hats and tales so fast.
The shells tell stories of mischief-made,
While seaweed crowns have friends parlayed.

A sunken boat, quite a sight,
With mermaids dancing in the light.
We cast our nets of silly dreams,
And chase the tide with giggly screams.

Echoes linger in salty air,
As waves wear secrets, unaware.
In hidden cove where laughter swells,
We weave our tales with coastal spells.

Gentle Hues of the Horizon

As dawn breaks with a whisk of gold,
A sleepy seagull starts to scold.
Crab runs past, what a sight!
Its morning hustle brings delight.

The waves roll in, a frothy show,
While sandcastles sway to and fro.
We chase the tide with squeals of glee,
As shells become our trophy spree.

Painted skies with hues divine,
As sun melts down, we sip our wine.
With tipsy laughs and sunset hues,
Our stories flow like ocean blues.

Each gentle wave whispers, "Stay!"
With sandy toes, we frolic and play.
In fleeting moments, joy takes flight,
In horizon's peace, our hearts unite.

Crabs and Crystals

A crab in a hat, quite dapper it seems,
Strolled along the shore, lost in his dreams.
He bumped into shells, quite shiny and bright,
Deciding then, they'd dance through the night.

The waves all applauded, a splashy encore,
As crabs shuffled sideways, felt like a chore.
With each little tiptoe, the sands they would tease,
While seagulls above laughed, enjoying the breeze.

Interludes on the Isle

A parrot once claimed he could sing opera high,
But all that he managed was a squawk and a cry.
A tourist then laughed, tried to join in the act,
But tripped on a rock and his flip-flop went slack.

The locals all chuckled, as the waves rolled in,
While the parrot just winked with a cheeky grin.
They danced on the sand, what a sight to behold,
With stories of blunders and laughter retold.

The Sweetness of Sea Grapes

Juicy and plump, in the shade they would grow,
Delight for the beach-goers, stealing the show.
A monkey swung by, with mischief in mind,
He snagged all the grapes, leaving none for his kind.

With sticky little fingers and a smile so sly,
He tossed down some grapes, as the seagulls flew high.
The laughter erupted, as fruits fell in heaps,
And down by the shore, a feast sprung from leaps.

Starry Nights and Swaying Trees

Under a sky where the stars twinkle bright,
A raccoon danced close, in the cool of the night.
He twirled with the palm fronds, a sight most absurd,
While critters around him all cheered, undeterred.

The moon played a tune, soft and sweet to the ear,
As the raccoon spun faster, showing no fear.
"Join in!" he called out, with a wild little wave,
And soon the whole beach was a party to save.

Lullabies of the Ocean Breeze

The seagulls sing their silly song,
While crabs dance like they can't be wrong.
A flip-flop flies, oh what a sight,
As friends just laugh and take flight.

The tide tickles toes like a playful pup,
While shells hide treasures, small and up.
A jellyfish floats, looking so proud,
While waves cheer on, forming a crowd.

Palm trees sway with graceful flair,
As coconut drinks spill everywhere.
We giggle, we shout, under the sun's glow,
In this ocean kingdom, we let laughter flow.

Night falls, but the fun's not done,
Starfish join in, everyone's having fun.
With a wink and a wave, they start to prance,
In lullabies we hum, we join the dance.

Driftwood Dreams

On the shore, driftwood lies in peace,
But to the crabs, it's an endless feast.
Each twig a throne, for a king to claim,
While everyone laughs at the driftwood game.

A mermaid giggles from her sandy chair,
In seashells she wears, with wind in her hair.
An octopus brings snacks to share,
Delicious seaweed, if you dare.

We race the waves, chase the foam,
Building castles, far from our home.
With sea spray kisses and sandy toes,
In this funny paradise, anything goes.

Night drapes its blanket, stars shine so bright,
And the driftwood dancers twirl with delight.
Each wave and laughter echo sweet,
In our coastal realm, we feel complete.

The Rhythm of Waves

The waves crash down with a comical cheer,
While clueless seagulls wander near.
Splashing friends with water balloons,
As mermaids giggle under the moon.

We skitter and scatter, avoiding seaweed,
Laughing at crabs with extraordinary speed.
Each splash a song, each wave a dance,
As we wade through silliness, given the chance.

Flip-flops fly, a showdown of sorts,
One lands on a fish, and now it reports!
The ocean's gossip travels far and wide,
From fish to gulls, there's nowhere to hide.

Stars twinkle bright as the rhythm plays on,
With dreams of tomorrow, and laughter 'til dawn.
Each wave carries tales of joy and fun,
In our seaside world, we're never done.

Sunsets and Seashells

The sun dips low in a peachy sky,
While rays tickle toes as we walk by.
Seashells giggle, they're having a blast,
Singing of tales from the ocean's vast.

We gather treasures, a whimsical spree,
Strange finds that make us laugh with glee.
A mismatched pair of flip-flops we find,
"Fashion statements," we all have in mind!

As the tide rolls in, we jump and shout,
While a wayward wave gives the beach a rout.
With laughter echoing, our joy is found,
In every sunset, magic is bound.

As night embraces, stars flicker bright,
With seashell whispers, and joy, we invite.
Each moment a treasure, a story to tell,
In the gallery of sunsets, we laugh so well.

Celestial Conversations by the Coast

The stars above twinkled bright,
While crabs danced under moonlight.
A parrot shouted, 'What a sight!'
'Is that a boat or a floating kite?'

Seagulls squawked in a silly tune,
'Join us for a midnight boon!'
Mermaids giggled, making a fuss,
As clowns in boats caused quite a fuss.

Shells whispered secrets in the sand,
'This is not the day we planned!'
A fish in a hat threw a wild grin,
'Life's a laugh, let the fun begin!'

And as they laughed beneath the stars,
They found that joy is never far.
So grab your friends, let's not be late,
For every night's a laughable fate!

Starry Nights and Salty Kisses

With a wink and a splash, a wave came near,
A fish joked, 'Here's your ticklish pier!'
'Put your toes in, don't be shy,'
The tide plays tricks, oh my, oh my!

Under the sky, a coconut fell,
A kid yelled, 'It's a tropical well!'
Laughter erupted, joy's in the air,
While a crab asked, 'Do we need a chair?'

Friends raced for the beach, oh what a sight,
Chasing sandcastles in the dark night.
'Who knew the tide could be this fun?'
'Let's dance with the waves and outshine the sun!'

Under the stars, we shared many tales,
Of jellyfish dances and playful gales.
With salty kisses and laughter so sweet,
These nights by the coast are truly a treat!

Tales of the Tropical Tide

A turtle set up a beachside shop,
Selling seashells and fizzy soda pop.
He winked at a crab with a sunhat bright,
'Join me for a drink, it's quite a sight!'

The waves rolled in with a comedic sigh,
'Why do you humans keep passing by?'
A dolphin splashed high, gave a playful leap,
As tourists chuckled, losing their sleep.

Under the palms, a party did sway,
With dancing fish in their own ballet.
Flamingos in shades, they strutted along,
With a chorus of crabs singing their song.

Raccoons raided snacks, oh what a scene!
They danced around in their messy cuisine.
With tales of the tide that giggle and spin,
This tropical life is where it begins!

Whispering Palms at Dusk

Under palm trees, the whispers grow,
Stories of sun and waves in tow.
A lizard laughed, 'Did you hear the tale?'
'Of the fish that danced, and a rainbow sail?'

The breeze carried secrets, soft and slick,
While an octopus played a ukulele lick.
The shadows twirled, making everyone grin,
And the ocean's chuckle was free feeling in.

A starfish called for a midnight show,
With jellybeans falling from somewhere below.
We all gathered 'round, in this sandcastle fair,
While the moon winked down, with a mischievous glare.

So let's share a laugh at the closing of day,
With whispers and giggles as we fade away.
These tales by the shore are our playful delight,
In the warm glow of dusk, oh what a night!

Island Legends Unfold

In the shade, the big crabs dance,
With silly moves, they take a chance.
The seagulls squawk, they join the fun,
Flapping wings 'til the day is done.

Tales of wise fish that wear big hats,
Swim by the boats, like friendly brats.
They tell their jokes, we laugh so loud,
Echoing tales beneath the cloud.

A surfer falls, and splashes wide,
The board flips over; oh, what a ride!
The coconuts laugh, they roll on the sand,
Joining the chaos as life's unplanned.

As night descends, the stars appear,
We sip our drinks, the smiles are near.
Island antics, a playful spree,
In these moments, we're wild and free.

Tidal Echoes

The waves come in with a mighty roar,
They tickle toes on the sandy shore.
A hermit crab races, a tactical pro,
He hides in a shell, putting on a show.

Seashells gather, gossiping tales,
Of fishy squabbles and gullish flails.
They chuckle as they bask in the sun,
In a world where random is loads of fun.

A beach ball bounces, off someone's head,
Laughter erupts; no tears to shed.
The tide rolls out, but humor stays,
As we chase bubbles in playful ways.

At dusk, the lanterns cast their glow,
Under giggling stars, we put on a show.
Stories arise from the shimmering sea,
Every splash a line in our laughter spree.

Beneath the Banyan

The banyan tree whispers, tales of old,
Of pirates and mermaids, both brave and bold.
A parrot squawks, making quite a scene,
As he juggles coconuts; what a routine!

Below its branches, friends gather round,
In the shade, we share what's profound.
The sun plays tricks, making shadows dance,
As we burst into laughter, given a chance.

A monkey swings by, snatching a snack,
Leaving us giggling, a comical act.
We roll on the ground, as laughter rings,
In the heart of the tree, joy always clings.

As the day fades, stories become myths,
About the monkey and his splendid gifts.
Amongst the roots, we weave our dreams,
In this playful world, laughter redeems.

Coral Reefs and Quiet Reflection

Underwater gardens teem with life,
Fish don bow ties, avoiding strife.
The clown fish giggles, with colors bright,
In the reef's embrace, everything's light.

A turtle strolls by, at his own pace,
With a sleepy grin on his wrinkled face.
He stops for a chat, a gentle guide,
In his slow-motion world, we take pride.

Jellyfish waltz, floating like dreams,
While sea cucumbers plot silly schemes.
They tickle the currents, laughter ensues,
In this watery realm, we shake off the blues.

As we swim back up to the sunlit shore,
We carry their echoes, laughter galore.
Reflecting on moments, joyful and free,
In the heart of the ocean, we find glee.

Secrets Beneath the Shoreline

A crab in a tux, oh what a sight,
Dancing on rocks beneath the moonlight.
Fish gossip loudly in bubbles and waves,
While a clam plays the rhythm of reckless braves.

A treasure map drawn by a cheeky gull,
With spoons for submarines in a bright blue hull.
Mermaids all giggle, they can't find their way,
Steering with seashells and laughing all day.

A parrot squawks jokes in a palm tree high,
While the tide brings in sandcastles to ply.
A starfish with dreams of a land dry and grand,
Waves a friendly goodbye, all washed up on land.

So let's raise a drink with an umbrella flair,
To the secrets that bubble just beneath the air.
With laughter so loud and the waves as our guide,
Let's dance by the shoreline with the tide by our side.

Sunlit Sands and Starlit Skies

On the sunlit sands where the seagulls dive,
Lies a crab with a hat, quite the jive.
He mimics the tourists with a silly grin,
While tourists retire, their sunburns begin.

Under starlit skies, the turtles race,
Wearing old sunglasses, they set the pace.
They giggle through shells, their laughter rings,
Making joyful sounds that only night brings.

A beach ball bounces in a misfit game,
With kids running wild, no one's to blame.
Flip-flops flapping in a comical beat,
As laughter erupts with each sandy retreat.

So gather around for this fun-filled show,
With tales of a world only sun lovers know.
Under stars and soft sands, let joy be the prize,
As hearts grow lighter beneath moonlit skies.

Echoes of the Island Breeze

In the whispering palms where the breezes play,
A coconut fell, rolling merrily away.
The hermit crabs chuckle, with shells in a whirl,
While they spin like ballerinas, oh what a twirl!

The breeze carries tales of a fish in a hat,
Who thinks he's the king and the world's his mat.
He waves to his subjects, the gulls in a row,
While they ponder his hobbies and put on a show.

At dusk, the sea foam gets tangled with tales,
Of sea turtles scheming and setting forth trails.
With fins in the air they declare with great glee,
That nothing can beat the life of the sea!

So come spin a laugh and dance with delight,
In echoes of breezes beneath the moonlight.
For each grain of sand holds a giggle or cheer,
In the heart of the island, where laughter is near.

Shells of Solitude

On a beach all alone with a shell as a friend,
A starfish named Fred did a rather odd blend.
He wore it like armor and walked quite absurd,
While crabs chuckled softly, oh what a word!

Building tall towers of sand with a grin,
They'd tumble each time as the waves swept them in.
A jellyfish jiggled, flinging around,
While a group of sea urchins sat on the ground.

As twilight approached with colors so bold,
The stars emerged shyly like stories untold.
Each creature would whisper their dreams made of light,
While the tide swayed to rhythms of fun in the night.

So let's cherish these moments, so silly and bright,
With shells of solitude that bring pure delight.
The beach holds its magic in laughter and glee,
Where every wave carries the secrets of the sea.

Journeys Through Salty Air

With a flip-flop lost, I take a chance,
The seagulls laugh, they start their dance.
A splash in the sand, my friend takes a dive,
We giggle and tumble, feeling so alive.

A crab in my shoe, oh what a sight,
He pinches my toe, it gives me a fright.
We chase the waves, our laughter is loud,
A typical day, feeling so proud.

Sunburned noses and sun-kissed skin,
Ice cream drips down, oh, where to begin?
We plan a feast, but snack on the way,
Who knew beach days could be so risque?

As fleeting as tides, our antics unfold,
Each moment a story, each tale worth gold.
We'll stow them in jars, memories to keep,
While night folds around, we'll drift into sleep.

A Tapestry of Tides

Waves roll in with a soft, funny sound,
Dancing around, trouble is found.
A bucket full of shells, a sticky surprise,
The crabs mock us, oh how they rise!

Paddle boards tip, and there goes the crew,
Land on the beach with no clue what to do.
Finding lost treasures, all sunburned and red,
With laughter and snacks, we're well-fed.

Seagulls steal fries, they swoop and they dive,
We yell in protest, trying to survive.
Each gull a pirate, cheeky and bold,
In the saga of fun, our antics unfold.

As daylight winks, we gather around,
With tales always changing, in laughter we're bound.
Under the stars, with a breeze in the air,
Our tapestry of tides, woven with care.

The Lure of Endless Horizons

Shells in our pockets, driftwood in hand,
We strut down the shoreline, feeling so grand.
With buckets and shovels, we dig to the core,
Only to find we've lost the sea lore.

A kite in the sky, then down with a flap,
Its tail in the sand gives us all a laugh.
The horizon whispers secrets untold,
We treasure each moment, more precious than gold.

A snack of fresh fruit, the juice drips in streams,
Nature's sweet bounty feeds our big dreams.
As laughter erupts, each friend takes a turn,
We share goofy tales while the sunset does burn.

With applauding waves, the tide has its say,
An endless horizon, where we play all day.
With smiles in our hearts, we're home on this shore,
The lure of adventure, we simply adore.

Fishermen's Whispers

Fishermen gather, tall tales they spin,
With nets full of laughter, let the fun begin.
A catch of the day, or just old seahorses?
Their stories of glory, oh where are the horses?

Worms wiggling fiercely, a noble affair,
They wiggle right out, sending us to despair.
An octopus sneaks in, wearing a grin,
We shriek and we stumble, can't help but give in.

With fish flopping wildly, the nets start to sway,
They dance on the deck in a slippery play.
Among all the chaos, friendship is found,
In the heart of the sea, laughter is loud.

As the sun dips below, they pack up their gear,
With hearts full of joy and a few too many beers.
Tomorrow we'll come, with rods in the sun,
For fishermen's whispers lead to barrel of fun.

Timeless Footprints in the Sand

Bobby ran fast, then tripped on a crab,
He swore it was chasing him, oh what a blab!
The tide washed his jokes away with a splash,
But laughter echoed as we all made a dash.

We built a sandcastle, tall like a tower,
It started to lean, oh no, we lost power!
A seagull swooped down, claimed our flag with glee,
We all just shrugged, 'It's his now, you see?'

Jenna lost her flip-flop, it flew like a kite,
The dog thought it's lunch, oh what a delight!
We chased it through waves, a slapstick ballet,
With laughter and splashes, we ended the day.

As shadows grew long, we danced like the waves,
Singing off-key, as the beach laughter saves.
Timeless the moments, written in sand,
With footprints of giggles shared hand in hand.

The Color of Coral

Underwater, we searched for treasures galore,
A fish dressed in colors we couldn't ignore.
It winked at us twice, then swam out of sight,
We chased it in circles, what a silly flight!

Bob found a shell that was shaped like a shoe,
He slipped it on, said, 'Oh, it fits like a tune!'
We laughed till we cried, a beach fashion show,
Our runway was sandy, and oh, did we glow!

Ellen tried surfing, ended up with a splash,
She paddled like crazy, what an epic crash!
The waves rolled in, teasing her with cheer,
But she stood up again, laughing without fear.

At sunset, the corals turned pink, orange, and gold,
We joined in a conga, feeling bold and uncontrolled.
Dancing with shadows, we'd twirl and we'd sway,
The ocean kept giggling, in its own funny way.

Sanctuary of the Salt Spray

The seagulls cawed, they had something to say,
'Pirate or chef? You can't serve fish today!'
A vessel of laughter rode waves of delight,
As waves rolled in, we'd giggle at height.

Maddie's hair tangled, a bird made a nest,
She claimed it was fashion, a beak and a jest.
We sprayed sunblock like warriors all brave,
But somehow got stuck, in our own sunscreen wave.

A sandbar appeared, and so did old Pete,
He offered us snacks, with a strange little tweet.
A pineapple hat? We all had a laugh,
Our picnic turned wild over chopstick and quaff.

The salt in the air danced like a fairy,
We sang silly songs till our voices were airy.
In this sanctuary, nothing seemed wrong,
Just tales of the beach, funny, light, and strong.

Memories Under the Palm Canopy

Under palm leaves swaying, we gathered like bees,
Telling wild stories, just as light as the breeze.
Clara claimed she saw a mermaid named Sue,
But everybody knew, it was old Uncle Lou.

We whispered of pirates and treasures well hid,
While munching on snacks like a well-fed kid.
A monkey appeared, stole our treat with a grin,
He danced on the branches, our laughter worn thin.

The sun dipped low, and the stories got tall,
We ventured in shadows, no fear of a fall.
'Two-headed fish!' cried Sam, as he made a sweet face,
And we all howled together, what a silly race!

At last, as we lounged, the stars shone so bright,
With memories sparkling, we laughed into night.
Under palm canopies, stories will weave,
A tapestry funny, that none will believe.

The Journey of Wayward Waves

Waves danced and played, how wild they roved,
Chasing the seagulls, not one was coved.
They whispered to crabs, who hid in their shells,
"Join in our frolic, we know the best dells."

From shore to the deep, they rolled and they crashed,
Tickling the sand, so gleefully splashed.
But every high tide turned laughter to sighs,
As beach umbrellas took off to the skies!

The rhythmic retreat, a graceful ballet,
Left shells chuckling softly at the end of the day.
A wise ol' turtle said, "Don't take it to heart,
For every good wave must eventually part."

So next time you stroll where the ocean does play,
Remember the waves in their funny display.
Join in with the surf, let your troubles float free,
And laugh with the sand, as bright as can be!

Tales Woven in Seafoam

In frothy white waves, secrets were spun,
Tangled with stories and giggles and fun.
The jellyfish jived, with elegance and flair,
While fish told tall tales of the octopus fair!

A crab donned a top hat, he skipped on the sand,
With a tip of his claws, he shouted, "A grand!"
The starfish clapped gently, the clams joined in song,
While the rogue tide rolled, just where it belonged.

Ladies and gents of the briny blue crew,
Gather 'round closely, there's much to construe.
Let every splash share a memory anew,
With laughter and cheetahs, all in one hue!

So if you should wander along the sea shore,
Look closely for whispers of tales made before.
For seafoam and joy will always unite,
In a carnival dance under soft, twinkling light.

Anemones and Afternoon Naps

Anemones swayed in the gentle sea breeze,
Whispered to hermits, "Let's do as we please!"
While sunbathers snored under wide, sunlit hats,
The fish tossed a party, complete with a spats!

They swirled in bright colors, all gleaming and flashy,
While everyone snoozed, they were quite splashy.
With bubbles for drinks and seaweed for snacks,
They danced with the laughter and left no tracks!

But soon on the tide, came a Snorlax so large,
He plopped on the beach, and took up the charge.
The party then halted as he snored with great might,
Turned fun into dreams, oh what a strange sight!

Yet when the moon rose, and the stars shone bright,
The creatures awoke, ready for night.
With giggles and splashes, loud feelings unwrapped,
What fun they had, without ever a map!

Shadows Beneath the Sun

Under the sun, shadows started to play,
A crab in a top hat led break-dance ballet.
The turtles all laughed as they joined in the fun,
In this silly circus, oh, everyone's spun!

Dune bunnies jived, with their big floppy ears,
Dancing around while forgetting their fears.
The sun smiled down on this amusing display,
As the breeze joined the mix, what a joyous heyday!

But just as they thought this was blissful and grand,
A seagull swooped down, seeking snacks from the sand.
The shadows all shrieked, and with leaps they did dart,
As laughter erupted, straight from the heart!

So remember, dear friend, when you stroll by the sea,
Embrace all the shadows that dance wild and free.
For under the sun, hilarity reigns,
In the world of the waves, let joy be your gains!

Serenades of the Siren's Call

There once sang a fish who was quite a tease,
Her bubbles would burst in the warm summer breeze.
She'd flirt with the nets, then swim out of sight,
Leaving fishermen grumpy, not catching a bite.

A crab on a log gave a wink and a grin,
He danced with the waves as the waves rolled in.
Collecting his bits of seaweed so fine,
He claimed them as jewels, boasting they were divine.

A gull flew in shouting, 'I've won the big race!,'
But tripped on a shell, fell flat on his face.
The fish and the crab laughed until they turned blue,
In the world of the waves, it's all friendship, it's true.

So every night, under the moon's silver glow,
They gather together, their laughter will flow.
For life on the waves has its ups and its downs,
But joy is found here, in this kingdom of clowns.

The Language of Seashells

A snail with a hat held a fancy crayon,
He sketched crazy doodles, quite the artsy con.
His buddies would chatter, 'What's going on here?',
'It's a gallery, friends! Come see with good cheer!'

A starfish named Fred found a seashell so round,
He tried to put it on, but it flipped and he frowned.
With laughter surrounding, he twirled on the sand,
'Fashion's a challenge with five arms at hand!'

A clam held a party, with snacks from the sea,
'We'll feast on the seaweed,' he decreed with glee.
But the lobster arrived and he pinched all the treats,
'No crustacean should party when there's shellfish to eat!'

The tide rolled in gently, the sun dipped so low,
As laughter erupted, gleeful and slow.
For in this wild chaos, friendships bloom fast,
In a language of shells, built to forever last.

Driftwood Dreams

A piece of old driftwood sat lonely and sad,
Wishing to be more than just weathered and bad.
A sea turtle came by, gave a wink and a grin,
'You're a throne for my dreams! Let the fun times begin!'

A crab climbed aboard, with a smile so wide,
'Join us for laughter, I'll be the guide!
We'll sail on the waves, like a ship with no crew,
With seaweed for sails and the sky as our blue.'

The driftwood, now cherished, began to feel light,
As fish jumped around, a glorious sight.
They danced in his shadow as the sun set low,
Creating a magic that sparked secret glow.

And though he was just a washed-up old log,
He found he could dream, with his friends like a fog.
In this fanciful moment, joy glimmered and gleamed,
For life is quite lovely, when shared with a dream.

Breezy Ballet of the Bay

The breeze took a twirl, like a dancer so spry,
Tickling the fishes that swam drifting by.
They swirled and they whirled, in a watery dance,
As shells clapped along, cheering with happy chance.

A dolphin with style, in a tutu so bright,
Flipped over the waves with an elegant flight.
Danced with the jellyfish, who jiggled in glee,
'An oceanic ballet, come join us!' said he.

The seagulls were judges, perched high on a rock,
They flapped their wings, keeping time with the clock.
And a conch-shell musician played tunes in a key,
That made all the creatures swim wild and feel free.

So if you perch near the bay at twilight,
Listen to whispers of laughter and light.
For in the soft breezes that waltz on the shore,
Life's funny ballet is a treasure to store.

The Secret Life of Tidal Pools

In a pool, a crab wears a hat,
Strutting like he's where it's at.
A starfish winks, it's quite the scene,
While seaweed sways, all dressed in green.

A clam tells jokes, but no one laughs,
Shells scatter bits of sandy gaffs.
Fish gossip in a curious chat,
"Who does he think he is? Just a brat!"

The sea anemones dance with flair,
Swaying softly, they don't care.
"Are those real pearls?" the oysters croon,
"Nope, just bits of moonlight and a tune!"

So come and peek, take a good look,
At this lively, salty storybook.
Each ripple holds a giggle or two,
In a world that's silly, bright, and new.

Hearts Adrift in the Breeze

A kite named Jerry floats up high,
With socks for wings, oh my, oh my!
He dips and dives, a silly sight,
Chasing seagulls in pure delight.

A beach ball rolls and tumbles wide,
While umbrellas dance, with the tide.
"Hey, don't blow away!" a towel shouts,
As laughter echoes, and joy spouts.

A crumply crab takes off to chase,
The jiggly jellyfish in the race.
But when they crash, it's quite the sight,
Splashing joy in their playful fight.

So let your heart float on the breeze,
Embrace the whimsy, if you please.
Each moment is a gift, it's true,
With giggles shared between me and you.

Vibrations of Vista and Voyage

The seagulls sing in chorus bright,
While pirates dance in the golden light.
A treasure map, oh what a jest,
Leads to a cupcake hiding in a nest!

The surfboards wait in a merry line,
Each wave brings stunts, oh what a time!
A dolphin spins, then takes a bow,
"What's next?" he asks, "Any tricks now?"

Two sandcastles high, they stand proud,
With moat and flag, they're quite the crowd.
But wait! A wave, it gives a shove,
The castles laugh, "We float like a dove!"

So take a ride where the sea meets sky,
In fun and folly, let spirits fly.
Each splash a song, each breeze a shout,
In this entertaining world, there's never a doubt.

Whims of the Wind

Wind whispers secrets, a playful tease,
Blowing hats from heads with ease.
It tickles your nose, swirls through your hair,
Swoops like a bird, it has flair!

A frisbee flies, a dance in the air,
Chased by laughter everywhere.
"The wind's plot thickens!" they all cheer,
As flip-flops stumble, with no fear.

A sand dune giggles, rolling around,
As kites burst free, joyfully unbound.
"Catch me if you can!" the breeze proclaims,
With sneak-thief glee, it plays its games.

So join the ride, let the wind spin tight,
In its whirls and twirls, find pure delight.
With smiles abound, both near and far,
In this land of breezy whimsy, we are the stars.

www.ingramcontent.com/pod-product-compliance
Lightning Source LLC
Chambersburg PA
CBHW050317100526
44585CB00016BA/1547